LITTLE BLUE BOOK NO. 938
Edited by E. Haldeman-Julius

French Tales of Passion and Cruelty

HALDEMAN-JULIUS COMPANY
GIRARD, KANSAS

FRENCH TALES OF
PASSION AND CRUELTY

CONTENTS

Page

FRENCH TALES OF
PASSION AND CRUELTY

THE LOST WORDS OF LOVE
By CATULLE MENDES

I

Once upon a time a very cruel fairy, pretty as the flowers, but wicked as the serpents who hide in the grass ready to spring upon you, resolved to avenge herself upon all the people of a great country. Where was this country? On the mountain or in the plain, at the shore of the river or by the sea? This the story does not tell. Perhaps it was near the kingdom where the dressmakers were very skilful in adorning princesses' robes with moons and with stars. And what the offence under which the fairy smarted? On this point also the story is silent. Perhaps they had omitted to offer up prayers to her at the baptism of the king's daughter. Be this as it may, it is certain that the fairy was in a great rage.

At first she asked herself whether she should devastate the country by sending out the thousands of spirits that served her to set fire to all the palaces and all the cottages; or whether she should cause all the lilacs and all the roses to fade; or whether she should turn all the young girls into ugly old women. She could have let loose all the four winds in the streets and laid low all the houses and trees. At her command fire-spitting mountains would have buried the entire land under a mass of burning lava, and the sun would have turned from his path so as not to shine upon the accursed city. But she did still worse. Like a thief leisurely choosing the most precious jewels in a case, she removed from the memory of men and women the three divine words:

"I love you."

And having wrought this affliction, she removed herself with a smile that would have been more hideous than the church of the devil had she not had the most beautiful rosy lips in all creation.

II

At first the men and women only half perceived the wrong that had been done them. They felt they lacked something, but did not know what. The sweethearts who met in the eglantine lanes, the married couples who talked confidingly to each other behind closed windows and drawn curtains, suddenly interrupted themselves and looked at each other or embraced. They felt, indeed, the desire to utter a certain customary phrase, but they had no idea even of what that phrase was. They were astonished, uneasy, but they asked no question, for they knew not what question to ask, so complete was their forgetfulness of the precious word. As yet, however, their suffering was not very great. They had so many other words they could whisper to each other, so many forms of endearment.

Alas! It was not long before they were seized

with a profound melancholy. In vain did they adore each other, in vain did they call each other by the tenderest names and speak the sweetest language. It was not enough to declare that all the bliss lay in their kisses; to swear that they were ready to die, he for her and she for him; to call each other: "My soul; My flame! My dream!" They instinctively felt the need of saying and hearing another word, more exquisite than all other words; and with the bitter memory of the ecstasy contained in this word came the anguish of never again being able to utter or to hear it.

Quarrels followed in the wake of this distress. Judging his happiness incomplete on account of the avowal that was henceforth denied to the most ardent lips, the lover demanded from her and she from him the very thing that neither the one nor the other could give, without either knowing what that thing was, nor being able to name it. They accused each other of coldness, of perfidy, not believing in the tenderness which was not expressed as they desired it should be.

Thus the sweethearts soon ceased to have their rendezvous in the lanes where the eglantines grew, and even after the windows were closed the conjugal chambers echoed only with dry conversations from easy-chairs that were never drawn close to each other. Can there be joy without love? If the country which had incurred the hatred of the fairy had been ruined by war, or devastated by pestilence, it could not have been as desolate, as mournful, as forlorn as it had become on account of the three forgotten words.

III

There lived in this country a poet whose plight was even more pitiful than the plight of all the rest. It was not that having a beautiful sweetheart he was in despair at not being able to say and to hear the stolen word. He had no sweetheart. He was too much in love with the muse. It was because he was unable to finish a poem he had begun the day before the wicked fairy had accomplished her vengeance. And why? Because it just happened that the poem was to wind up with "I love you" and it was impossible to end it in any other way.

The poet struck his brow, took his head between his hands, and asked himself: "Have I gone mad?" He was certain he had found the words that were to precede the last point of exclamation before he had commenced to write the stanza. The proof that he had found them was that the rhyme with which it was to go was already written. There it was—it waited for them, nay, called aloud for them; it wanted no others, waiting for them like lips waiting for sister lips to kiss them. And this indispensable, fatal phrase he had forgotten; he could not even recall that he had ever known it. Surely there was some mystery in this, the poet mused unceasingly and with bitter melancholy—oh, the pang of interrupted poems!—as he sat at the edge of the forest near the limpid fountains where the fairies are wont to dance of an evening by starlight.

IV

Now as he sat one morning under the branches of a tree, the wicked, thieving fairy saw him and loved him. One is not a fairy for nothing; a fairy does not stand on ceremony. Swifter than a butterfly kisses a rose she put her lips on his lips, and the poet, greatly pre-occupied though he was with his ode, could not help but feel the heavenliness of her caress. Blue and rose diamond grottos opened up in the depths of the earth, luminous as the stars. Thither the poet and the fairy were drawn in a chariot of gold by winged steeds who left the earth in their flight. And for a long, long time they loved each other, forgetful of all but their kisses and smiles. If they ceased for a moment to have their mouths united and to look into each other's eyes, it was but to take pleasure in more amiable diversions. Gnomes dressed in violet satin, elves attired in a misty haze, performed dances before them that fell in rhythm with the music of unseen orchestras while flitting hands that had no arms brought them ruby baskets of snow-white fruit, perfumed like a white rose and like a virgin bosom. Or, to please the fairy more, the poet recited, while striking the chords of a therobo, the most beautiful verses his fancy could conceive.

Fairy that she was, she had never known joy comparable to this of being sung by a beautiful young man who invented new songs every day. And when he grew silent, and she felt the breath of his mouth near her, felt it passing through her hair, she melted away in tenderness.

Their happiness seemed without end. Days passed by, many, many days, but nothing occurred to disturb their joy. And yet she had moments of gloom, when she would sit musing, with her cheek on her hand and her hair falling in streams down to her hips.

"O queen!" he cried, "what is it that makes you sad; what more can you desire, seeing that we are so happy in the midst of all our pleasures, you who are all powerful, you who are so beautiful?"

At first she made no answer, but when he insisted, she sighed and said: "Alas! one always ends by suffering the evil that one has inflicted on others. Alas! I am sad because you have never told me: 'I love you.'"

He did not pronounce the words, but uttered a cry of joy at having found again the end of his poem. In vain the fairy attempted to retain him in the blue and rose-diamond grottos, in the gardens of lilies that were as luminous as the stars. He returned to earth, completed, wrote and published his ode, in which the men and women of the afflicted country found again the divine words they had lost.

Now there were rendezvous again in the lanes, and warm, amorous conversations at the conjugal windows.

It is because of poetry that kisses are sweet, and lovers say nothing that the poets have not sung.

A MARRIED COUPLE

By Marcel Prévost

All the Parisians who frequented Nice and Monte Carlo last season remembered having seen at the Circle, at the English promenade, at the theatre or at the races, the curious couple, whom Paul B—— had christened "lovers from beyond the grave." Indeed they made me think of spirits from a supernatural land of love. She, still young and very beautiful, gave this impression because of her emaciated form, the pallor of her face, and the æsthetic indifference of her splendid blue eyes; he, because of something, youthful, and hopelessly worn out that was betrayed in his nervous and depressed walk, and the carriage of his head, at once enfeebled and proud. Although he was getting gray he would have been handsome if not for the large black band which covered his right eye, and the upper part of his right cheek, not quite concealing the burns which seared the whole side of his face. Hand in hand these two beings would sit, and listen to the music, and breathe in the perfumes, and gaze at the far horizon, in the delightful fairyland, never mingling with the bustling noisy crowds which surrounded them. They were never seen with friends, and they did not seem to desire any, happy doubtless in the miniature universe which each was for the other. At nightfall, they would disappear; few people knew their retreat. They lived in a handsome villa, on the shore of the gulf, in Villi-franchi-Mer, right near the unpretentious house where I was staying. They were known as M. and Mme. Le Thierrey.

I came to know them merely by chancing to be their neighbor. The young woman, whose lungs were weak, used to leave the terrace where they dined early tête-à-tête. Many a time her husband and I would remain together smoking cigarettes, and lost in one of those silent reveries, or one of those leisurely conversations which the serene vastness of the views there inspires. And one evening it came about that he told me their story—without my soliciting his confidence—on an evening when the air, milder than usual, heavy with the scent of African flowers, or the greater calm of the sea —like molten copper beneath the broad rays of the moon, awoke in us both the desire to speak low, and to tell or hear tales of love.

"You have surely guessed," Le Thierrey said to me, "that there is a drama in Lucy's past and in mine; a commonplace tragedy, if one considers only the action itself, but rare and unusual perhaps because of its causes and its consequences.

"I am thirty-two years old; my wife is tweny-six; she was seventeen when I met her. She had come to live in Paris with her mother and her older sister. They lived on the fifth floor of the house and we were on the first. The life of these three women was, as happens in many provincial bourgeois households, abruptly broken up by a spoiled child's caprice. Lucy developed an irresistible bent for the stage, and since she did as she pleased with her mother and her sister Clémence, being so pretty and bright, so egoistic and so wilful, she made them decide to live in Paris, where they thought, she would burst forth as an artist and a celebrity by the mere effect of the artistic atmosphere of the city.

"At this time I left the École des Chartes. My life till then had been divided between study and the affection of my family. I was a kind of precocious savant, timid and with an untouched heart. I fell in love with Lucy at first sight. From that day, whatever other women could offer me meant nothing to me; and actually even now, I am so indifferent to feminine beauty that I do not know it when I see it.

"The girl realized the state of my feelings, and promptly began to make me suffer. In our furtive meetings on the stairs—meetings which I managed at the cost of great inconvenience, watching for her return from the Conservatory; in those meetings when I passed close to her, my heart failing me, scarcely finding strength to greet her, she pretended to pass without seeing me, or rather, what was still more cruel, she contrived to be taken home by her class-mates, with their smooth, sallow, bluish cheeks; taking their arms with every appearance of tenderness the moment she saw me. Apart from this, she remained impregnable, stubbornly indifferent to love, as unkind to others as to me.

"Luckily my passion had two advocates in Lucy's mother and sister. These two, whose one aim in life was the glory and happiness of their idol, immediately dreamed of a marriage which would make her rich, and give her as a husband a man of good family who adored her. You can imagine what struggles I had with my family, on account of this marriage. As for the girl, she would never have consented, had not repeated failures, first in the Conservatory, and then in several small trial scenes in which she made her début, disgusted her with the stage, and inspired her with the desire to wipe out all these humiliations by means of a brilliant marriage, which would humiliate her companions in their turn.

"I quarrelled with my family. I married Lucy. Her mother and elder sister lived with us.

"Till then, I had only to suffer the usual agonies of those who pursue a woman, who is beloved and cruel, over a thousand obstacles. But it was after possessing her that I became truly wretched. Lucy did not refuse herself to me; she managed something worse than that. As she gave herself to me, she declared haughtily that my caresses were odious to her, that she endured them because she felt herself obliged to, having sold herself to me for my fortune and my name. When she spoke like this, I was forced to admit to myself that she was not lying. In the eyes of my wife I stood for her lost career, her vanished artistic glory. I was the living permanent proof of the crumbling of her dreams.

"The burden of deception which she loaded upon all who surrounded her, bore most heavily on me, whom she could hurt most because I was the one who loved her most. Oh! the baseness of desire! I endured all, her coldness, her disdain, her insults, so long as she gave me her beloved body, whose possession became more dear, the more degradation it cost me. I had convinced myself that my life was united to an exception soul, with a sort of pathological perversity, possessed by egoism and malice, and the desire to give pain; and this soul I still adored and still fondly hoped to win over into adoration of me.

"I will not retrace with you the stages of my Calvary. All that pride and tenderness of a husband could suffer, I suffered. I am a man, sir, to whom his wife said one day, 'I am going to betray you, not because I love another, but because I hate you and want to dishonor you. And she did so. She betrayed me with an individual worthy of the utmost contempt. And I did not part from her; I went on adoring her."

Le Thierrey stopped speaking. It was quite dark by now. In the profound silence we heard nothing but the slashing of the wavelets, and the hushed notes of a piano from the closed windows of the villa. For a moment my companion listened to the music. He murmured with an expression of ineffable tenderness:

"The Pastoral Symphony! It is she who is playing!"

After a few more moments of silence he went on:

"My mother-in-law died the year following my marriage, but my sister-in-law, Clémence, kept on living with us. She was my one consolation. No one could better understand and sympathize with my misery than this poor girl

whose whole life had been a voluntary sacrifice
to the woman I had chosen for my companion.
We did not need to confide in each other to
know each other's sad secret. The day Lucy
broke the last barrier, and left me to go to
live with a lover, only Clémence was able to
keep me from killing myself.

"I lived. . . . We remained, the elder
sister and I, guardians of the empty hearth,
like two old people whose only child was dead.
The world at once declared that we were lovers.
It was false, it was mad—need I say so? Our
aching souls were utterly closed to love. But
the world does not understand how a young
man and a young woman can associate in order to weep together. The talk of gossipings
was brought to us; we were counselled to put
an end to our unequivocal situation. We paid
no attention and continued living as before.
Together, at least, we could talk of Lucy. And
then, what did these idle remarks matter to
us? Were we not two beings retired from the
world?

"Here comes the drama of which I spoke
to you. This drama, I told you, is commonplace in itself; so I will tell it to you in a few
words. Lucy heard that I was her sister's
lover. Why did this woman, who did not love
me and who was betraying me, at once conceive a jealousy so sharp as to suggest a crime
to her? I suppose that she was exasperated
by the thought that the two beings whom she
had tortured could afford each other the su-
preme consolation. It was the period when
several sensational trials had made vitriol
fashionable. One evening as Clémence and I

were returning home arm in arm from a melancholy walk, a woman hidden behind the corner of the house suddenly unmasked herself and hurled at us the contents of a vial full of vitriol. Clémence was burned on the face and breast. She died next day in horrible convulsions. I was only sprinkled on the right temple, but I lost my eye and remained scarred for life.

"Have you heard, monsieur, of those cases of madness or idiocy cured by a fall, by a violent shock to the head?

"There took place in the soul of Lucy a miracle comparable to these in suddenness and completeness. This soul, like that of Lorenzaccio de Musset, was pregnant with a crime, but one crime only. Once it was committed she suddenly became once more an ordinary human soul, pitiful and suffering. It was as sudden and final as an exorcism. Seeing us fall she threw herself on our bodies, weeping and denouncing herself, calling for help in a terrible fit of despair. In prison she had to be constantly watched in order to prevent her from killing herself. And when, by accusing myself and the innocent memory of her sister (who, I am sure, pardoned her for it), I succeeded in securing her acquittal, it was she who tended me with incomparable devotion, and who saved my life at the risk of her health.

"These events are several years old; but since then, the reconquered tenderness of my wife has never diminished. At the same moment that her heart opened to pity and to love, her body revived to caresses. What

more shall I tell you, monsieur? I have de-
liberately forgotten the past; I love and am
loved; these words contain all. I am dis-
figured and infirm for life; most of my family has broken away from me; those of my
former friends who did not openly abandon
me, pitied me or despised me; doctors tell me
that my life will be short, and I sometimes
feel in my wound a recurrence of terrible pain.
But Lucy is mine; at last she belongs to me,
body and heart; I regret nothing; I have not
paid too dearly for my happiness."

My companion ceased to speak. Noises had
stopped, and the fires were out in the villa;
the piano was silent. Only the mysterious voice
of the sea broke the stillness. And without
a word, lost in reflection, he continued to gaze
upon that still, trembling ocean, so often com-
pared to the soul of woman.

LOVE IN THULE

By Maurice Barrès

In Seville, the city of her birth, Violante scandalized everybody by her beauty and her indiscretions. For at twenty she had the romantic habit of becoming a sister to the handsomest, most spirited and noble youths of her circle. She believed, quite mistakenly, of course, that if one's sentiments were lofty and one's conduct irreproachable one could afford to ignore all malicious gossipings. After being insulted several times she left Spain, first marrying a young Frenchman, who paid for the marriage with his health and his career.

They traveled for three years, then settled down in Paris, and at the end of her twenty-fifth year she was left a widow.

Her husband's family had not accepted her with very good grace, for despite their distinguished name they were people of a bourgeois mind, who looked upon every foreign women as somewhat of an adventuress; and this young woman was not the sort of person to make them believe the contrary. And so, when she was left alone, they did nothing to aid her in keeping up her position in society, where her largeness of soul, a thousand reports from Spain concerning her, and her rare charm soon placed her in a compromising position. It happened, moreover, that she accepted the devotion of a young man, as one is happy to do at that age.

No one knew anything very definite about

their relations, but as usual, people took the opportunity of thinking the worst. They were right. The important thing is that the pair treated one another during this liaison, which lasted for eight years, with infinite tact and delicacy. Nor did they purposely hurt one another, but on the contrary they ennobled one another by proving in their relations, that not everything is base and vulgar in this world. Thus they lived, he with nothing to occupy him, devoted and grateful; she, haughty and capricious towards the indifferent, all tenderness and devotion towards him. Marriage did not tempt them for a moment; it would have meant to introduce the element of obligation into the habits which they adopted without over much formality.

They met each other in society, at the theatre, and at the races, and almost every day they spent long hours together in their apartment in the Avenue Montaigne. The young woman slipped by insensible degrees from the best circles into male society alone, and seemed to be content with it. As for him, he never wearied of hearing her recount the adventures which had befallen her in Seville and in the course of her travels.

She told him of the wild asses in Africa, of the magnificent fruits in Andalusia, of the climate in the Balearic Isles: she found Italy a trifle insipid after her rugged Spain, she detested England, and cared nothing for Central Europe with the exception of the summer evenings in the Carlsbad restaurants, where the gypsies, known there as "Lothars," used to sing. He was in accord with her in respect to all these matters, and enjoyed immensely the picturesqueness and vividness of the sensations and impressions which she communicated to him with the manner of a blasé child.

She took special delight in a romantic conception of life, which she had long ago evolved and which she loved so much that she absolutely refused to allow herself to be disillusioned of this young girl's dream; it would have been a splendid sort of existence, she said, to form a perfect friendship, as between brother and sister, with young men of very refined sensibilities and to live in an atmosphere of pleasure, beauty and mutual trust, like children overflowing with life, who kiss each other and share their toys. And he, amidst these daring fancies of hers, which had, after all, somewhat lowered his moral tone, experienced a peculiar pleasure, very subtle and very profound, in pitying this being made up of optimism, sweetness and sensuality. His mind, moreover, grew keener in following her, for she judged things without regard to morality, but only according to the dictates of her sense of beauty and her passion for refinement.

However, he did not see complete happiness in the face of this beloved friend. Did she perhaps desire more violent emotion, did she believe herself not perfectly loved? He would question her sometimes.

"No," she would answer, "I am not suffering, but it seems to me that there is no joy that I have not already experienced."

He clasped her in his arms without a word, for he felt she was right. Splendid horses, the most humble of admirers, everything that the most meticulous snobbism might exact—all these she had, and now there was nothing more for her to take pleasure in, not even at her dressmakers. In a word, she was suffering from having exhausted all sensations.

One idea to which she frequently kept reverting, was that of visiting the countries of the far East, and he understood very well that she had built up an image of them from Japanese vases, brocaded silks and certain amusing figures at the Chinese legation, a purely legendary conception utterly devoid of everyday reality. It was the one experience which this fanciful person had not made trial of. She believed in China, not having had the occasion to see that there too existed that element of imperfection which detracts from everything that inheres in all reality. She often said:

"When I grow old, my beloved, and feel myself utterly incapable of enjoying the things which I possess, I shall go down there, send you gifts, and die."

As she had in her as much romantic feeling as a person can well possess without actually descending to the ridiculous, this pleased her—to end her life mysteriously, and to drown herself in the crowd, just as a little sick animal drowns itself in the Seine. Ah! to die, on a blazing day, practically abandoned, in a hotel in Shanghai, and by her end compel the mercy of God!

At last, the feeling of blankness from which they suffered became so great that she judged that the moment had come when they ought to separate, and though he felt that neither could any longer contribute to the happiness of the other, nevertheless his suffering was great, for it brought home to him definitely that their happiness was at an end. She told him of her painful intention, and then avoided discussion of it. This was partly out of consideration, and partly in order that his pleadings might not weaken her resolution. By a tacit agreement, they made a pretense of treating her undertaking merely as a trip to the countries of the East. Only the last time that they saw each other, in the apartment where they had lived through so much, they were terribly agitated. In the ante-room, dim in the closing day, near the door which for years had been for them a door to a universe apart, and which was now to be, they thought, only the entrance to a tomb, they united in a long embrace; not at all as a lover and his mistress, but of two beings of the same race who were met upon earth and who had never been hypocritical with each other.

"Promise me," she said to him, "that you will come here again sometimes. Always preserve our home, and let every trifle remain as we are leaving it today. If any woman chances to please you, do not have the least scruple about bringing her here, provided that she be a true friend, for my one wish is that you should be happy. But one evening, Christmas eve, I ask you to remain alone in this apartment."

She thought that on Christmas great mysteries took place in nature; that on that night, things acquired souls, and became alive.

"Promise me," she repeated, "that you will come and think of our former joy amidst all the things that used to surround us."

She spoke with so much tenderness, in a tone so purified of all the pangs of jealousy, that both of them felt the bitter pleasure of the devotee, although they did not know to what or to whom they devoted themselves, and their eyes filled with tears. Ah! how wretched they felt at their impotence to give joy to one another, and perchance ashamed to find happiness only in their grief!

He did as she wished, and in that apartment, given over to silence, he came at irregular intervals to spend an hour calling up the images of the past? Although she had promised to write to him, and to give him her successive addresses, he received no word from the traveller. For the rest, if he suffered, it was a delicious melancholy, a sort of "pleasure in self-torture," in thinking that he had let his fair treasure, his beloved, be drawn into the whirlpool.

Now, when eight months had passed, and Christmas was approaching, a chest filled with precious objects from China, was delivered one day in the Rue Montaigne. He put off opening it. Then on the night, when, in order to celebrate the birth of the Infant Jesus, the faithful embrace in the churches, and the *viveurs* in the cabarets, he shut himself up in their favorite room.

The lamps, set in their wonted places, shed upon the same decorations those lights and shadows, amongst which he and Violante had

passed so many evenings. Dressing-room and
music-room, upon both of them was the spell
of the sweetness of their intimacy and the
memory of impassioned music. It was in this
spacious room that he had been intoxicated
with tenderness and beauty, and for him it
was filled with a luminous and ardent atmosphere, like the voice of Van Dyck in the love-
song of Siegmund. It was there, at the knees
of his mistress, that little by little he had dis-
covered beneath the mask of the woman of
the world, the real woman, not at all a being
made up of social graces and pretty ways, but
instinct with humanity, and still very close to
the little girl who used to play with dolls.
That piano, those large mirrors, that dressing-
room, those vast wardrobes so gay with rib-
boned lingerie, were not merely inanimate objects, but friends, well-beloved companions;
those smelling-salts, which she played with
while talking together, which she so often
pressed to her appealing face, that blue vase
in which she delighted to arrange the yellow
tulips flecked with red and green, which went
by the droll name of "parrot tulips," all the
dainty fripperies, with which she had amused
herself, all those toys for grown-ups—everything had taken on a certain spiritual quality,
something which might almost have been called
a soul, by the fact that it had known the
caress of her touch, her glance, and her voice
so tender with love. In her hands and beneath the breath of her young mouth, the
flowers lived as though they actually were
gentle living creatures; they were no more
than vegetables now that the beloved one who

animated them with her loving kindness was
no longer there.

Little by little the objects began to speak
with him. . . . First the great three-panelled
mirror before which she had instinctively fallen
into graceful poses, shadowed forth her beauty.
"It is here," he said to himself, "when I ad-
mired the variety, the versatility, the thousand
aspects of her charm, that beauty came to seem
a living thing to me, the sum of a human
being's usefulness. Violante gave me a dis-
taste for museums and libraries, where things
are motionless and barren. It is through her
that I learnt the rather humid sensuality of
beauty, and for me she replaced also the for-
ests and the ocean and the splendor of night
in the wilderness. For I possessed their frag-
rance, their infinity, and their melencholy, according as her hair was loosened in little-girl
fashion, and her eyes drowned in bliss beneath
my lips.

"Here are the dressing tables and the familiar objects which she would not let me
touch, hastening to serve me herself, because
it amused her, she said, but, I knew well, in-
fluenced by a deeper motive, by the voluptuous
joy of self-humiliation—she, who was so charming, that she might love the better.

"It was at this window through which the
light streamed so brightly, that I sometimes
turned my eyes away from her face, on days
when her features looked drawn, and her expression fatigued, not at all because the circles
around her eyes were disagreeable to me—
something left to desire in her would have
made me love her the more—but because I

feared lest, conscious of her momentarily les-
sened beauty, my looking at her should make
her suffer.

"And here is the immense armchair, where
we passed the first hours, always so forced,
of our liaison. Outside, it was a sad snowy
afternoon; in us were mingled feelings of desire and calculation. But one day, two months
later, when the first fire had spent itself, she
uttered the profound truth at last—the occasion was a tactless remark with which she had
offended me—which touched the very core of
existence more decisively than all the words
of love, and even than the first *tutoiment* on
dying lips. A terrible utterance, which makes
a solemn affair of a caprice, and transforms
those between whom it passes. How can I
recreate the impassioned tone, the vibrant
voice with which she said, slipping into my
arms, 'In love, my dearest, there is no self-
respect.' "

A saying of too strong a flavor, sensual as
vice, and which, wrong from a creature of in-
toxicating finesse and grace, demoralizes all
one's being more than twenty years of de-
bauchery. Under that apparent nobility of
sincere feeling, what a vessel in which to
drown all the dignity of a man and all his
pride! Love teaches disinterestedness, it is
true; but it cuts us off from the best as well
as from the worst. Sad and bitter summing-
up! The conventional order of things, crime,
humiliation, physical imperfection, nothing
more had any meaning for these two who
henceforth knew nothing in the world outside
of themselves. In the mass of laws which

rule all human beings love takes the place of pledges; it interprets everything in its own terms and breaks the chains of honor in order to bind us together as accomplices.

These are the memories which the room where he had lived through all these sweet moments with Violante brought back to the young man. Thus the profound feeling and the taste for life, and without any repugnance for untrammeled desire, the freedom from all formalities, this is what these friendly objects gave back to him, these backgrounds to their love, on Christmas Eve when things inanimate can speak to the soul.

Did he regret his beloved? Not at all. "For her to remain with us longer," he said to himself, "would have been too much, for we were surfeited; she could not have given us any more. Whereas now, although she is absent, everything which we could drink in from her soul dwells on in these things and in me. The millions of beings and things which today are dead, which make beautiful the forest, the going down of the sun, and the words of speech—each of these, having contributed its share to the enrichment of the universe, has nothing to do but die—and thus Violante has enriched us and left us.

"But Violante having enriched by herself the object of her love and these inanimate things has not yet played her role to its end. She has not yet expended all her vital force. Little unwearying seed, she has entrusted herself to the wind. She has gone to bear her soul across the sea."

At that moment he thought of the tokens

which Violante Had sent him from far distant
countries—coffers filled with cold, mysterious
trinkets, in which were placed kind thoughts
of the traveller together with many tender
memories. One by one he lifted out and han-
dled the vases, the silks and the bronzes;
vainly he essayed to surprise their secret, and
make them to speak to him on this Christmas
eve.

"Among the thousand of objects down there
in the bazaars, Violante has chosen these. She
has chosen them, as she chose me, and as we
chose so many pleasures with common accord;
but these strangers can tell me nothing. She
went toward them, she understood them immediately and I do not understand them at all.
Could it be possible that we were two beings
living the same life, mingling our thoughts, so
that even the most delicate nuances seemed
gross and superfluous, and nevertheless her
instincts sighed for things which for me had
no meaning?" Then he recalled that sometimes she saw in her dreams grimacing forms,
fantastic and terrible, which troubled her and
which she would not treat as mere nightmares.
She delighted in embroidering, in the beautiful
garments in which her ardent spirit slumbered,
dragons, unicorns, the phenix, and the tortoise,
which are the dream animals of the East. And
descending further into the spirit of the exile,
who often on summer evenings had tears of
joy in her beautiful eyes, he recovered to
memory the vibrating tones with which she
used to describe with glowing words, the
scent of roses, and death, in the narrow streets
of Cordova. Thus this woman and temptress,

formed to create life, loved all which made
for disintegration, as if she would have joyed
more in her beauty amongst dying things, and
would rather have established her reign among
the forces of decomposition.

All these wrappings filled the apartment with
the decaying odor and the deadly fever which
breathes from the grave.

"At this hour, doubtless," he dreamed, "in
that country where decay is swiftest she has
exhausted her nervous force and breathed away
her entire soul. She has satisfied her bound-
less prodigality in lavishing upon these Chinese several aspects of her being with which
I have never been able to come into contact.
Perhaps, too, as I may think without conceit,
she has transmitted to them much that she has
gathered from me. Her task is ended. According to her vow, this coffer appears before
me as a sign of her death. I have not the
strength to combat the blow which these events
are giving me. Although we were near to each
other during these years, our destinies were
separate. I shall not grieve; there is already
descending forgetfulness, the dust which effaces —
individual forms. I am rather disgusted to see
that my feelings are like a thin string of
curious pearls which dance on a loose thread.
Well it was that we played music in this
room! It raised for a paradise beyond time
and space, where our desires, mingling at moments, gave us the illusion that our being
was one."

And now, having seated himself at the piano
in the first light of that sad Christmas morning the young man hummed the love-song of

Siegmund, thinking that perhaps in some hotel in the Orient she was choosing this night on which to die—this night when she knew that he was living over their past, and mingled with his grief at her death, the clear vision of the immutable ways of the world aroused in him a feeling of impotence and bitterness. Bitter distress to see how few were the grains loosened from the sand on the bank by the ripples set circling by the vessel which fell into the whirlpool of Thule.

THE RETURN

By Charles-Louis Philippe

He had waited till evening. At about a
quarter to seven he knocked at the door. A
voice, which he did not immediately recognize,
called out—"Come in." Without having to
grope for it, he found the latch in the old
place, raised it, opened the door and entered.

His wife was not surprised. Each knock at
the door, during the four years of his ab-
scence, had always made her think, "Perhaps
that's he coming back." She had a soup-
tureen on her lap and was holding a loaf
against her breast; she was slicing bread for
the soup with a motion that was very familiar
to him. Without a word, she placed the tureen
and the bread on a chair, then, lowering her
head, she clutched at her apron and covered
her face. He did not have to see her eyes to
know that she was weeping.

He sat down, leaned against the back of his
chair and not finding anything to say, looked
the other way. He was utterly at a loss.

The three children were hanging over the
table around the lamp. The two little ones,
Lucien and Marguerite, were playing lotto.
They saw that a man had come in; a man
like all the rest who came and talked of things
which did not interest children. They went on
with their game. But Antoinette, the oldest,
who by now was almost thirteen, and who was
busy writing her lessons, her exercise-book wide

open before her, recognized him almost immediately, despite his beard, and cried, "Oh! It's papa!"

She had grown very much. She still had those little tricks on account of which he had loved to tease her, because she had always been so ready with some amusing rejoinder. She could not continue her work. She got up and, as he had his back turned, she placed her hand on his shoulder. He waited no longer, but looked around at her. She was not timid. She considered him triumphantly and said, "It's a long time since you have called me the fruit of your love!" She had always treasured that in her heart. When they had all lived together, he had hung around the inn all day long. He was a farrier by trade, but when a customer came to have a horse shoed, his wife had to send Antoinette for her father. Whenever he saw the child coming for him among the drinkers, he would turn to his companions, saying, "Here's my daughter, gentlemen, my eldest daughter, the fruit of my love!" Each time this would make her furious.

He passed his hand over her hair, but did not dare to kiss her yet. Just at this moment the door opened at the push of a new arrival. Baptiste Pondet, a carpenter, came in with such assurance, that Larmingeat understood everything without any explanations. He rose as one rises when the head of the house comes in, and said: "Yes, you see it's me." Baptiste answered, "Sit down." Then he added, "I am like your wife; I always thought you would come back." Then as they were men, and men know life, they did not keep silent long. Larmingeat said, "Do you think I have made a blunder?" Baptiste Pondet explained in turn:

"Good Heavens! my good fellow! I—I've lost my wife."

"Ah! she's dead, that poor Adele."

"Yes, and I tell you it was all over quickly. It was an inflammation of the lungs, lasting three days. I had lost the habit of being alone. She's a good woman, your wife."

Larmingeat answered:

"As for me, what do you want? I had so many debts and no work. I thought they didn't need a drunkard round the house. I left to get a job, I said—But I might have written to her."

"Yes, at the end of three months, she understood that you had left her. Well, everyone has his faults."

They were silent for a minute. They knew each other well, these two. They were of the same class, they had served together in the 36th Artillery, at Clermont-Ferrand. Larmingeat remembered it and said, "Who would have thought of this when we were in the army."

Such was the return of Larmingeat. Such were the words he said.

Tears cannot last forever. The woman lowered the apron with which she was covering her face, and then she took hold of the tureen and the bread to go to an adjoining room, which served as kitchen. Antoinette also, seeing that she did not understand what was going on in the room, ended by joining her.

The two men remained alone, facing each other, and Larmingeat said: "I see that it would have been better for me not to return."

Baptiste Pondet answered, "Well, all right, but you had to know what had happened to your wife and your children."

They were very kind to him, as he sat shifting restlessly about on his chair, and seeming anxious to take his leave, like a person who has no reason for staying. Baptiste Pondet said to him:

"But you will remain for supper with us?"

He accepted because he could not do anything else. He could not go to the inn, for this was his home town. His wife, Alexandrine, who had somewhat recovered her confidence, heard Baptiste and was of the same opinion. She put her head through the doorway, not to make any remark, but merely to observe that there was only some soup and cheese and that that was little enough. Baptiste was a good fellow. He declared that they ought to get some pork and a bottle of wine. Larmingeat, not wishing to be behind, brought out twenty sous. He insisted on paying for his bottle and said, that if there was any change, they should buy sweets for the children. Then he added for politeness' sake:

"I am putting you to some expense."

The children removed their lotto-game quickly when they learned that someone was dining with them. They were well pleased and wished to set the table. Alexandrine brought out a tablecloth which she placed on the table. Larmingeat objected, but she said, "Goodness, I have it; I may as well use it when there's

company." When she returned with a small
ham, some brawn, the two bottles and cakes,
they began the meal. Larmingeat was very
hungry. He avowed it without ceremony, and
the few words he uttered were sufficient to
set the conversation going.

They asked him how he managed things,
where he slept, where he took his meals. It's
true, he had not even told them that he
came from Paris. He slept in a hotel. He
ate in a restaurant. The hardest thing was to
get someone to mend his clothes. He worked
at the Metropolitan as the subway is called.
He explained what the Metropolitan was. Baptiste said:

"Yes, they do all sorts of work."

They made a good meal of it. Langevin
senior was no longer the pork-butcher, but his
son's meat was very good also. The two bottles were used up. If Alexandrine had not
said that she was not thirsty, there would not
have remained enough wine for the cheese.
Only one thing had been forgotten—cigars.
But Larmingeat took out his purse once more,
and gave ten sous to Antoinette, saying, "There,
my child, get us two cigars." She was a charming child. She not only went willingly, but
wanted her father to come with her; she would
have walked him through the town. Her
mother had to say to her, "Come on now, leave
your father alone, and be careful not to tell
the clerk that it's for him. No one has to
know that he is here."

There was a fairly sad moment a little
later when the children were being put to

bed. It was easy enough with the little ones who were practically asleep at table. Larmingeat gave them two sous each, but they would not say, "Thank you, papa." They said, "Thank you, sir." When it was Antoinette's turn, she threw herself on her father. It seemed as if she had been quiet till then only to reserve her strength and to cry with more emotion. "I don't want him to go away. I don't want him to go away." She clung to his neck. Her mother said, "Look now, you are hurting him."

They were obliged to pull her away by force, tear her from him and promise that he would not go away. Larmingeat wept and Alexandrine and Baptiste wept with him. When she was gone, Baptiste said, "You saw that child? Well, there's not a better to be found. I have always been sorry that she is not mine."

When the children were in bed, everybody began to yawn; it was getting so late. All the cigars had been smoked. As there was not a drop to drink, they had nothing to do. Larmingeat knew what he had to do. He said, "Well, I suppose I've got to go."

They did not keep him back. They merely asked him how he had come. He had come by train. He even told them that he had brought his valise along because at first he had wanted to stay. His wife said:

"Heavens, you should not have left the first time. What can you expect? I had to settle down. I cannot keep on marrying and unmarrying all the time. However, it turned out well."

There was a train at eleven. The station

was six kilometers away and it would not do
to be late as the train did not wait. Before
he went, Baptiste, in one of those moments in
which one sums up all that one has said, re-
marked:

"You see how things are with us? My fur-
niture is here, there is one bed more than in
your time."

He showed him the arrangement of the
rooms. The landlord had made some repairs.
He led him into the children's room. The
walls had been papered and the chimney, which
used to smoke, had been fixed. The children
were tight asleep. Larmingeat did not dare
to kiss them, for fear of disturbing their sleep.
He said, "I see that you are really comfort-
able."

He kissed Alexandrine before leaving, then
as Baptiste stretched out his hand, he said,
"Come, old fellow, let us kiss, too."

THE IDYL OF AN OLD COUPLE

By PIERRE LOTI

Toto-San and Kaka-San were husband and
wife. They were old—so old; everybody had
always known them; the oldest people in Naga-
saki did not even remember the time when they
had seen them young. They begged in the
streets. Toto-San, who was blind, dragged after
him in a sort of small bath-chair Kaka-San,
who was paralyzed. Formerly they were known
as Hato-San and Oume-San (Monsieur Pigeon
and Madame Prune), but the people no longer
remembered this. In the Japanese language
Toto and Kata are very soft words which sig-
nify "father" and "mother" in the mouths of
children. Doubtless because of their great age,
everybody called them so; and in this land of
excessive politeness they added to these familiar names the word "San," which is a word
of courtesy like monsieur and madame (*Monsieur Papa* and *Madame Maman*). Even the
smallest Japanese babies do not neglect these
terms of politeness. Their method of begging
was discreet and *comme il faut*. They did not
harass the passers-by with prayers, but held
out their hands simply and without saying
anything—poor hands, wrinkled and already
like those of a mummy. The people gave them
rice, heads of fish, old soups. Very small,
like all Japanese women, Kaka-San appeared
reduced almost to nothing in this chair, in
which her lower limbs, almost dead, had been

dried up and huddled together for so many years. Her carriage was badly hung; and thus it came to be much jolted in the course of its journeys through the city. He did not walk very quickly, her poor husband, and he was so full of care and precaution. She guided him with her voice, and he, attentive, his ear pricked up, went on his way, like the Wandering Jew, in his everlasting darkness, the leather rein thrown over his shoulder and striking the ground with a bamboo cane to direct his steps.

They went to all the religious festivals celebrated in the temples. Under the great black cedars, which shade the sacred meadows, at the foot of some old monster in granite, they installed themselves at an early hour before the arrival of the earliest devotees, and so long as the pilgrimage lasted, many of the passers-by stopped at their side. They were young girls with the faces of dolls, and little eyes like cats, dragging after them their high boots of wood; Japanese children, very funny in their long parti-colored dresses, arriving in bands to pay their devotions and holding each other by their hands; beautiful simpering ladies, with complicated chignons, going to the pagoda to pray and to laugh; peasants with long hair, Bonzes or merchants, every imaginable description of these gay little doll-people passed before Kata-San, who still was able to see them, and Toto-San, who was not. They always gave them a kind look, and sometimes somebody would detach himself from a group to give them some alms. Sometimes even they made them bows, quite as if they were people of quality—so

well were they known, and so polite is everybody in this Empire.

In those days it often happened that they
could smile at the feast when the weather was
fine and the breeze soft, when the sorrows of
old age slumbered a little in their exhausted
limbs. Kaka-San, excited by the tumult of the
laughing and light voices, began to simper like
the passing ladies, playing with her poor fan
of paper, assuming the air of one who still
had something to say to life, and who interested herself like other people in the amusing
things of this world.

But when evening came, bringing darkness
and chill under the cedars, when there was
everywhere a sense of religious horror and
mystery around the temples, in the alleys lined
with monsters, the old couple sank back on
themselves. It seemed as if the fatigues of the
day had gnawed them from within; their
wrinkles became deeper, their skin hung more
loosely; their faces expressed only their frightful misery and the hideous idea of the nearness
of death.

Meantime, thousands of lamps were lit
around them in the black branches; and the
devout held their places on the steps of the
temples. The hum of a gayety, at once frivolous
and strange, came from this crowd, filled the
avenues and the holy vaults, in sharp contrast
with the sinister grin of the immobile monsters
who guard the gods—with the frightful and unknown symbols—with the vague terrors of the
night. The feast was prolonged till daylight,
and seemed an immense irony to the spirits of
heaven rather than an act of adoration; but an

irony that had no bitterness, that was child-like
amiable, and, above all things, irresistibly
joyous.

But this affected not the old couple. With
the setting of the sun there was nothing which
could animate any longer those human wrecks.
They became sinister to look at; huddled up,
apart from everybody else, like sick pariahs or
old monkeys, worn out and done for, eating in
a corner their poor little alms-offerings. At
this moment were they disturbed by something
profound and eternal, else why was there this
expression of anguish on their death-masks?
Who knows what passed in their old Japanese
heads? Perhaps nothing at all. They struggled
simply to keep on living; they ate with their
little chop-sticks, helping each other tenderly.
They covered each other up so as not to get
cold and to keep the dew from penetrating to
their bones. They took care of each other as
much as they with the simple desire of being
alive the next day, and of recommencing their
old wandering promenade, the one rolling the
other's chair. In the little chair Kaka-San kept
all their household effects, broken dishes of
blue porcelain for their rice, little cups to drink
their tea, and lanterns of red paper which they
lit at night.

Once every week, Kaka-San's hair was carefully combed and dressed by her beloved husband. Her arms she could not quite raise high
enough to fix her Japanese chignon, and Toto-
San had learned to do it instead. Trembling
and fumbling, he caressed the poor old head,
which allowed itself to be stroked with coquet-
tish abandon, and the whole thing recalled—

except that it was sadder—the toilette which the humbugs help each other to make. Her hair was thin; and Toto-San did not find much to comb on her poor yellow parchment, wrinkled like the skin of an apple in winter. He succeeded, however, in fixing up her hair in puffs, after the Japanese fashion: and she, deeply interested in the operation, followed it with her eyes in a broken piece of a mirror, with: "A little higher, Toto-San." "A little more to the right." "A little to the left." In the end, when he had stuck two long pins in, which gave to the coiffure its finishing touch, Kaka-San seemed to regain the air of a genteel grandmother, a profile like that of a well-bred woman.

They also went through their ablutions conscientiously: for they are very clean in Japan.

And when they had finished these ablutions once more, which had been done so often already during so many years; when they had completed that toilette, which the approach of death rendered less grateful from day to day— did they feel themselves vivified by the pure and cold water? did they experience a little more comfort in the freshness of the morning?

Ah! what a depth of wretchedness was theirs! After each night, to wake up both more infirm, more depressed, more shaky, and in spite of it all, to wish obstinately to live on, to display their decrepitude to the sun, and to set out in the same eternal promenade in their bath-chair; with the same long pauses, the same creaks of the wood, the same joltings, the same fatigue; to pass even through the streets, into the suburbs, through the valleys, even to the distant country where a festival was announced in some temple in the woods.

It was in the fields one morning, at the crossing of two of the Royal roads, that death suddenly caught old Kaka-San. It was a beautiful morning in April; the sun was shining brightly, and the grass was very green. In the island of Kiu-Tiu the spring is a little warmer than ours, comes earlier, and already everything was resplendent in the fertile fields. The two roads crossed each other in the midst of the fields; all around was the rice-crop glistening under the light breeze in innumerable changes of colour. The air was filled with the music of grasshoppers, which in Japan are loud in their buzz. At this spot were about ten tombs in the grass under a bunch of large and isolated cedars. Square stone pillars, or ancient Buddhas in granite, were set up in the cups of the lotus. Beyond the fields of rice, you saw the woods, not unlike our wood of oak. But here and there were white or rose-coloured clumps, which were the camelias in flower, and the light foliage of the bamboos. Then farther off were the mountains, resembling small domes with little cupolas, forming against the sky shapes that seemed artificial, yet very agreeable.

It was in the midst of this region of calm and verdure that the chair of Kaka-San stopped, and for a halt that was to be its last. Peasants, men and women, dressed in their long dresses of dark blue cotton with pagoda sleeves—about twenty good little Japanese souls—hurried to the bath-chair where the old dying woman was convulsively twisting her old arms. She had had a stroke quite suddenly while being drawn along by Toto-San on a pilgrimage to the temple of the goddess Kwanon.

They, good souls, did their best, attracted by sympathy as much as by curiosity, to help the old woman. They were for the most part people who, like her, were making their way to the feast of Kwanon, the Goddess of Beauty. Poor Kaka-San! They attempted to restore her with a cordial made of rice brandy; they rubbed the pit of her stomach with aromatic herbs, and bathed the back of her neck with the fresh water of a stream. Toto-San touched her quite gently, caressed her timidly, not knowing what to do, embarrassing the others with his awkward, blind movements, and trembling with anguish in all his limbs.

Finally, they made her swallow, in small pellets, pieces of paper which contained efficacious prayers written on them by the Bonzes, and which a helpful woman had consented to take from the lining of her own sleeves. Labour in vain! for the hour had struck. Death was there, invisible, laughing in the face of all these good Japanese, and holding the old woman tight in his secure hands.

A last painful convulsion and Kaka-San was dead. Her mouth lay open, her body all on one side, half fallen out of the chair, and her arms hanging like the doll of a poor Punch and Judy show, which is allowed to rest at the close of the performance.

This little shaded cemetery, before which the final scene had taken place, seemed to be indicated by the Spirits themselves, and even to

have been chosen by the dead woman herself.
They made no delay. They hired some coolies
who were passing, and very quickly they began
to dig out the earth. Everybody was in a
hurry, not wishing to miss the pilgrimage nor
to leave this poor old thing without burial—
the more so as the day promised to be very hot,
and already some ugly flies were g..thering
round. In half an hour the grave was ready.
They took the old woman from her chair, lift-
ing her by the shoulders, and placed her in the
earth, seated as she had always been, her lower
limbs huddled together as they had been in
life—like one of those dried-up monkeys which
sportsmen meet sometimes at the foot of trees
in the forest. Toto-San tried to do everything
himself, no longer in his right senses, and
hindering the coolies, who have not sensitive
hearts, and who hustled him about. He groaned
like a little child, and tears ran from his eyes
without exciting any attention. He tried to
find out if at least her hair was properly
combed to present herself in the eternal dwell-
ings, if the bows of her hair were in order
and he wished to replace the large pins in her
head-dress before they threw the earth over her.

They heard a slight groaning in the foliage;
it was the spirits of Kaka-San's ancestors who
had come to receive her on her entrance into
the Country of Shadows. Toto-San yoked himself to the bath-chair once more; once more
started out, from the sheer habit of walking
and of dragging something after him. Sepa-
rated from her who had been his friend, adviser,
his intelligence and his eyes, he went about
without thought, a mournful wreck, irrevocably

alone on earth to the very end, no longer
capable of collecting his thoughts, moving
timidly without object and without hope, in
night blacker than ever before. In the meantime the grasshoppers sang at their shrillest
in the grass, which darkened under the stars;
and whilst real night gathered around the old
blind man, one heard already in the branches
the same groanings as earlier while the burial
was taking place. They were the murmurs of
the spirits who said: "Console thyself, Toto-
San. She rests in a very sweet sort of anni-
hilation·where we also are and whither thou
com'st soon. She is no longer old nor totter-
ing, for she is dead; nor ugly to look upon,
since she is hidden in the roots underground:
nor disgusting to anybody, since she has become the fertilizing substance of the land. Her
body will be purified, permeating the earth:
Kaka-San will live again in beautiful Japanese
plants; in the branches of the cedar, in the
beautiful camelias—in the bamboo."

LASTING LOVE

By GUY DE MAUPASSANT

It was the end of the dinner that opened the hunt. The Marquis de Bertrans with his guests sat around a brightly lighted table, covered with fruits and flowers. The conversation drifted to love. Immediately there arose an animated discussion, the same eternal discussion as to whether it were possible to love more than once. Examples were given of persons who had loved once; these were offset by those who had loved violently many times. The men agreed that passion, like sickness, may attack the same person several times, unless it strikes to kill. This conclusion seemed quite incontestable. The women, however, who based their opinion on poetry rather than on practical observation, maintained that love, the great passion, may come only once to mortals. It resembles powder, they said, this love. A heart once touched with it becomes forever so void, so ravaged, so consumed, that no other strong sentiment can find rest in it, not even a dream.

The Marquis, who had indulged in many love affairs, disputed this belief.

"I tell you it is possible to love several times with all one's heart and soul. You quote examples of persons who have killed themselves to prove the impossibility of a second passion. I wager that if they had not foolishly com-

mitted suicide and so destroyed the possibility
of a second experience they would have found
a new love and still another and so on till
death. It is with love as with drink. He who
has once indulged is forever a slave. It is a
thing of temperament."

They chose the old Doctor as arbitrator. He
thought it was as the Marquis had said, a thing
of temperament.

"As for me," he said, "I once knew of a love
which lasted fifty-five years without one day's
respite, which ended only with death." The
wife of the Marquis clasped her hands.

"That is beautiful! Ah, what a dream to be
loved in such a way! What bliss to live for
fifty-five years enveloped in an unwavering,
penetrating affection! How this happy being
must have blessed his life, to be so adored!"

The Doctor smiled.

"You are not mistaken, Madame, on this
point—the loved one was a man. You even
know him; it is Monsieur Chonquet, the chem-
ist. As to the woman, you knew her also, the
old chair-mender, who came every year to the
Château." The enthusiasm of the women
fell. Some expressed their contempt with
"Pouah!" for the love of common people did
not interest them. The Doctor continued:
"Three months ago I was called to the death-
bed of the old chair-mender. The priest had
preceded me. She wished to make us the ex-
ecutors of her will. In order that we might
understand her conduct, she told us the story
of her life. It is most singular and touching.

Her father and mother were both chair-menders. She never lived long in any one place. As a little child she wandered about with them, dirty, unkempt, hungry. They visited many towns, leaving their horse, wagon and dog outside the limits, where the child played in the grass alone until her parents had repaired all the broken chairs in the place. They seldom spoke, except to cry, 'Chairs! Chairs! Mender of chairs!'

"When the little one strayed too far away, she would be called back by the harsh, angry voice of her father. She never heard a word of affection. When she grew older, she fetched and carried the broken chairs. Then it was she made friends with the little street urchins, but their parents always called them away and scolded them for speaking to the bare-footed mender. Often the boys threw stones at her. Once a kind woman gave her a few pennies. She saved them most carefully.

"One day—she was then eleven years old—as she picked her way through a country town she met, behind the cemetery, the little Chonquet, weeping bitterly, because one of his playmates had stolen two precious pennies. The tears of the small villager, one of those much-envied mortals, who, she imagined, never knew trouble, completely upset her. She approached him and, bowing, asked the cause of his grief, and put into his hands all her savings. He took them without hesitation and dried his eyes. Wild with joy, she kissed him. He was busy counting his money, and did not object. She, seeing that she was not repulsed, began again to kiss him and even gave him a tremendous hug—then she ran away.

"What was going on in her poor little head? Was it because she had sacrificed all of her fortune that she became madly fond of him, or was it because she had given him her first tender kiss? The mystery is alike for children and for those of riper years. For months she dreamed of that corner near the cemetery and of the little villager. She stole pennies from her parents to give him at their next meeting. When she returned to the spot near the cemetery, he was not there. Passing his father's drug store, she caught sight of him behind the counter. He was sitting between a large red globe and a blue one. She only loved him the more, and, wrought up to an ecstasy by the sight of him surrounded by the brilliant-colored globes, she nearly fainted with emotion. She cherished forever in her heart this beautiful sight. The following year she met him near the school, playing marbles. She threw herself on him, took him in her arms, and kissed him so passionately that he cried aloud. To quiet him, she gave him all her money. Three francs! A real gold mine, at which he gazed with staring eyes.

"After this he allowed her to caress him as much as she wished. During the next four years she put into his hands all her savings, which he pocketed conscientiously in exchange for kisses. At one time it was thirty sous, at another two francs. Again, she only had twelve sous. She wept with grief and shame, explaining brokenly that it had been a poor year. The next time she brought five francs, in one whole piece, which made her laugh with joy. She no longer thought of any one but the boy, and he watched for her with impatience; sometimes he would run to meet her. This made her heart thump with joy. Suddenly he disappeared. He had gone to boarding-school. She found this out by careful investigation. She soon ingratiated herself with his parents and used her diplomacy in order that they might call him home for the holidays. After a year of intrigue she met with success. She had not seen him for two years, and scarcely recognized him. he was so changed, tall, beautiful and dignified in his uniform, with its brass buttons. He pretended not to know her, and passed by without a glance. She wept for two days and since then loved and suffered until the end.

"Every year he returned and she passed him, not daring to lift her eyes. He never condescended to turn his head toward her. She loved him madly, hopelessly. She said to me:

" 'He is the only man whom I have ever seen. I don't even know if another exists.' Her parents died. She continued their work.

"One day, on entering the village, where her heart always remained, she saw Chonquet coming out of his pharmacy with a young lady leaning on his arm. She was his wife. That night the chair-mender threw herself into the river. A drunkard passing the spot pulled her out and took her to the drug store. Young Chonquet came down in his dressing-gown to revive her. Without seeming to know who she

was, he undressed her and rubbed her; then
he said, in a harsh voice:
"'You are mad! People must not do stupid
things like that.' His voice brought her to life
again, and she was happy for a long time. He
refused remuneration for his trouble, although
she insisted.

"All her life passed in this way. She worked, thinking always of him. She began to buy
medicines at his pharmacy; this gave her a
chance to talk to him and see him closely. In
a way, she was still able to give him money.

"As I said before, she died this spring.
When she had closed her pathetic story she
entreated me to take her earnings to the man
she loved. She had worked only that she
might leave him something to remind him of
her after death. I gave the priest fifty francs
for her funeral expenses. The next morning I
took the rest to Monsieur Chonquet as he was
finishing his breakfast. His wife sat at the
table, fat and red, important and self-satisfied.
They welcomed me and offered me some cof-
fee, which I accepted. Then I began my story
in a trembling voice, sure that they would be
softened, even to tears. As soon as Chonquet
understood that he had been loved by that
vagabond! that chair-mender! that wanderer!'
he swore with indignation, as though his repu-
tation had been sullied, the respect of decent
people lost, his personal honor, something
precious and dearer to him than life, gone.
His exasperated wife kept repeating: 'That
thing! That thing!'

"Seeming unable to find words suitable to

the enormity, he stood up and began striding about. He muttered: 'Can you understand anything so horrible, Doctor? Oh, if I had only known it while she was alive, I should have had her thrown into prison. I promise you she would not have escaped.'

"I was dumfounded; I hardly knew what to think or say, but I had to finish my mission. 'She commissioned me,' I said, 'to give you her savings, which amount to three thousand five hundred francs. As what I have just told you seems to be very disagreeable, perhaps you would prefer to give this money to the poor.'

"They looked at me, that man and woman, speechless with amazement. I took the few thousand francs from out of my pocket. Wretched-looking money from every country. Pennies and gold pieces all mixed together. Then I asked:

" 'What is your decision?'

"Madame Chonquet spoke to me first. 'Well, since it is the dying woman's wish, it seems to me impossible to refuse it.'

"Her husband said, in a shamefaced manner: 'We could buy something for our children with it.'

"I answered dryly: 'As you wish.'

"He replied: 'Well, give it to us anyhow, since she commissioned you to do so; we will find a way to use it for some good purpose.'

"I gave them the money, bowed and left.

"The next day Chonquet came to me and said brusquely:

" 'That woman left her wagon here—what have you done with it?'

" 'Nothing; take it if you wish.'

" 'It's just what I wanted,' he added, and walked off. I called him back and said:

" 'She also left her old horse and two dogs. Don't you need them?'

"He stared at me surprised: 'Well, no! Really, what would I do with them?'

" 'Dispose of them as you like."

"He laughed and held out his hand to me. I shook it. What will you? The doctor and the druggist must not be at enmity. I have kept the dogs. The priest took the old horse. The wagon is useful to Chonquet, and with the money he has bought railroad stock. That is the only deep, unfailing example of love that I have ever known in my whole existence."

The Doctor looked up. The Marquise, whose eyes were full of tears, sighed and said:

"There is no denying the fact, only women know how to love."

INDISCRETION

By Guy de Maupassant

They had loved each other before marriage with a pure and lofty love. They had first met by the seashore. He had found this young girl charming, as she passed by with her light-colored parasol and her dainty dress clearly outlined against the horizon. He had loved her, blond and frail, in this impressive frame of blue ocean and azure sky. He could not distinguish the tenderness which this budding woman awoke in him from the vague and powerful emotion which the fresh salt air and the grand scenery of surf and sunshine and waves stirred up in his soul.

She, on the other hand, had loved him because he courted her, because he was young, rich, kind, and attentive. She had loved him because it is natural for young girls to love men who whisper sweet nothings to them.

So for three months they had lived side by side and hand in hand. The greetings which they exchanged in the morning before the bath, in the freshness of the new-born day, or in the evening on the sand, under the stars, in the warmth of a calm night, whispered low, very low, already had the flavor of kisses, though their lips had never met.

Each dreamed of the other at night, each thought of the other on awakening, and, without yet having voiced their sentiments, each longed for the other, body and soul.

After marriage their love descended to earth. It was at first a tireless, sensuous passion, then exalted tenderness composed of tangible poetry, very proper caresses, and new and foolish inventions. Every glance and gesture was an expression of passion.

But, little by little, without even noticing it, they began to get tired of each other. Love was still strong, but they had nothing more to reveal to each other, nothing more to learn from each other, no new tale of endearment, no unexpected outburst, no new way of expressing the well-known, oft-repeated verb.

They tried, however, to rekindle the dwindling flame of their first love. Every day they tried some new trick or desperate attempt to bring back to their hearts the uncooled ardor of their first days of married life. They tried moonlight walks under the trees in the sweet warmth of the summer evenings, the poetry of mist-covered beaches, the excitement of public festivals.

One morning Henriette said to Paul:

"Will you take me to a café for dinner?"

"Certainly, dearie."

"To a well-known café?"

"Of course!"

He looked at her with a questioning glance, seeing that she was thinking of something which she did not wish to say.

She went on:

"You know, one of those cafés—oh, how can I explain myself?—in a sporty café!"

He smiled: "Of course, I understand—you mean in one of the cafés which are commonly called Bohemian."

"Yes, that's it. But take me to one of the big places, one where you are known, one where you have already supped—no—dined—well, you know—I—I—on! I will never dare say it!"

"Go ahead, dearie. Little secrets should no longer exist between us."

"No, I don't dare."

"Go on; don't be prudish. Tell me."

"Well, I—I—I want to be taken for your sweetheart—there! and I want the boys who do not know that you are married, to take me for such; and you too—I want you to think that I am your sweetheart for one hour, in that place which must hold so many memories for you. There! And I will play that I am your sweetheart. It's awful, I know—I am abominably ashamed, I am as red as a beet. Don't look at me!"

He laughed, greatly amused, and answered:

"All right, we will go tonight to a very swell place where I am well known."

Toward seven o'clock they went up the stairs of one of the big cafés on the Boulevard, he smiling, with the look of a conqueror, she timid, veiled, delighted. They were immediately shown to one of the luxurious private dining rooms, furnished with four large arm-chairs and a red plush couch. The head waiter entered and brought them the *menu*. Paul handed it to his wife.

"What do you want to eat?

"I don't care; order whatever is good."

After placing his coat in the hands of the waiter, he ordered the dinner and called for champagne.

The waiter looked at the young woman and smiled. He took the order and murmured:

"Will Monsieur Paul have his champagne sweet or dry?"

"Dry, very dry."

Henriette was pleased to hear that this man knew her husband's name.

They sat on the couch, side by side, and began to eat.

Ten candles lighted them, and were reflected in the mirrors all around the room, which seemed to increase the brilliancy a thousand-fold.

Henriette drank glass after glass in order to keep up courage, although she already felt dizzy after the first few glasses. Paul, excited by the memories which returned to him, kept kissing his wife's hands. His eyes were sparkling.

She was feeling strangely excited in this new place, restless, pleased, a little ruffled, but full of life. Two waiters, serious, silent, accustomed to seeing and forgetting everything, to moving only when it was necessary and to leaving when they felt that they were superfluous, were silently flitting hither and thither.

Toward the middle of the dinner, Henriette was well under the influence of champagne. She was prattling along fearlessly, her cheeks flushed, her eyes glistening.

"Come on, Paul; tell me everything."

"What, sweetheart?"

"I don't dare tell you."

"Go on!"

"Have you loved many women before me?"

He hesitated, a little perplexed, not knowing whether he should hide his adventures or boast of them.

She continued:

"Oh! please tell me. How many have you loved?"

"A few."

"How many?"

"I don't know. How do you expect me to know such things?"

"Haven't you counted them?"

"Of course not."

"Then you must have loved a good many!"

"Perhaps."

"About how many? Just tell me about how many."

"But I don't know dearest. Some years a good many, and some years only a few."

"How many a year, did you say?"

"Sometimes twenty or thirty, sometimes only four or five."

"Oh! that makes more than a hundred in all!"

"Yes, just about."

"Oh! I think that is dreadful!"

"Why dreadful?"

"Because it's dreadful when you think of it —all those women—and always—always the same thing. Oh! it's dreadful, just the same— more than a hundred women!"

He was surprised that she should think that dreadful, and answered, with the air of superiority which men take with women when they wish to make them understand that they have said something foolish:

"That's funny! If it is dreadful to have a hundred women, it's dreadful to have one."

"Oh, no, not at all!"

"Why not?"

"Because with one woman you have a real bond of love which attaches you to her, while with a hundred women it's not the same at all. There is no real love. I don't understand how a man can associate with such women."

"But they are all right."

"No, they can't be!"

"Yes, they are!"

"Oh, stop; you disgust me!"

"But then, why did you ask me how many sweethearts I had had?"

"Because——"

"That's no reason!"

"What were they—actresses, little shop-girls, or society women?"

"A few of each."

"It must have been rather monotonous toward the last."

"Oh, no; it's amusing to change."

She remained thoughtful, staring at her champagne glass. It was full—she drank it in one gulp; then putting it back on the table she threw her arms around her husband's neck and murmured in his ear:

"Oh! how I love you, sweetheart! how I love you!"

He threw his arms around her in a passionate embrace. A waiter, who was just entering, backed out, closing the door. Service was interrupted for about five minutes.

When the head waiter came back, solemn and dignified, bringing fruits and dessert, she was once more holding between her fingers a full glass, and staring down through the amber liquid as though seeing unknown things. She murmured in a dreamy voice:

"Yes, it must be fun!"

OTHER LITTLE BLUE BOOKS
OF FRENCH LITERATURRE

(ALL TITLES ARE IN ENGLISH)

Guy de Maupassant

6 Love, and Other Stories.
292 Mademoiselle Fifi, and Other Stories.
199 The Tallow Ball (Boule de Suif).
886 The Piece of String, and Other Stories.
887 The Necklace, and Other Stories.
915 Mad, and Other Stories.
916 A Night in Whitechapel, and Other Stories.
917 Room Number Eleven, and Other Stories.
918 The Man With the Blue Eyes, and Other Stories.
919 The Clown, and Other Stories.
920 A Queer Night in Paris, and Other Stories.
921 Madame Tellier's Establishment, and Other Stories.
922 A Wife's Confession, and Other Stories.

Honoré de Balzac

15 The Atheist's Mass and an Accursed House.
143 Time of the Terror, and Other Stories.
318 Christ in Flanders, and Other Stories.
344 Don Juan and a Passion in the Desert.

Gustave Flaubert

570 Legend of St. Julian the Hospitaller.
617 Hamilcar: Great Man of Carthage.

Anatole France

198 The Majesty of Justice.
219 The Human Tragedy.
828 The Wisdom of the Ages, and Other Stories.
707 Epigrams of Love, Life, and Laughter.

Theophile Gautier

178 One of Cleopatra's Nights.
230 The Fleece of Gold.
345 Clarimonde: A Supernatural Passion.

Remy de Gourmont

540 Stories of Many Hues.
541 Brightly Colored Tales.
377 A Night in the Luxembourg.
582 Philosophic Nights in Paris.

George Sand

196 The Marquise.
106 Thoughts and Aphorisms.

Victor Hugo

27 Last Days of a Condemned Man.
104 The Battle of Waterloo.
379 The King Enjoys Himself (Drama).

Moliere (Drama)

99 Tartuffe.
134 The Misanthrope.
229 Les Precieuses Ridicules.
309 Nobody Who Apes Nobility (Le Bourgeois Gentilhomme).

These titles are selected from several hundred Little Blue Books now available; a complete catalog may be obtained, on request, from

HALDEMAN-JULIUS COMPANY
Girard, Kansas

CPSIA information can be obtained
at www.ICGtesting.com
Printed in the USA
BVOW06s0427120817
491859BV00012B/119/P